THE LITTLE BOOK ON FORGIVING

THE LITTLE BOOK ON FORGIVING

A Surrender in 7 Steps toward Peace and Freedom

RICK KITZMAN

DeVorss Publications

The Little Book on Forgiving
Copyright © 1998
by Rick Kitzman

ISBN: 0-87516-714-4
Library of Congress Catalog Number: 97-78004
Second Printing, 2000

DeVorss & Company, Publisher
P.O. Box 550
Marina del Rey, CA 90294

Printed in The United States of America

Forgiveness is not an occasional act;
it is a permanent attitude.

DR. MARTIN LUTHER KING, JR.

This book is about change.
Your change.
If you are not ready to change, have the courage to admit it.
Put this book down and pick it up when you so wish.
If you are ready to change, have the courage to proceed.
Whichever choice you make is perfect for you.

Change is inevitable except from
vending machines.

AUTHOR UNKNOWN

Contents

My Story

The purpose of this book is to help you heal. You are such an important and beautiful part of our world that when you heal, the world heals.

For me to write this book, I had to heal.

During the summer of 1981, on a Brooklyn rooftop overlooking the Manhattan skyline, good friends and I topped off a wonderful dinner with chocolate chip cookies, strawberries, and kiwis. It was my first time tasting the cool, green fruit. It was also the first time I heard about some strange disease affecting gay men. The serenity and contentment of the evening palled as each of us tried to comprehend the implications of this news, so naïve and blind we were. I lay awake all night wondering if I was infected. So did the others. Life would never be the same for me, for my friends, this country, this planet.

Flash forward to a year later—the third week of August 1982, to be exact. An abnormally chilly week cooled the usually hot and humid air of New York City. This is the week that brought the need not for air conditioning and iced drinks and nude sleeping, but for blankets, hot tea, and jammies. This is the week I woke up in the middle of three nights lying in sweat-drenched sheets. This is the week I know—as I know my own name—that I became symptomatic with hiv (*sic*).* And this is the week that changed my life drastically and for the better, forever.

Anyone can tell you that when you discover the disease you have contracted is 100 percent fatal (and at the time, mine was), that news does a real number on your head, not to mention what it is doing to your body. Combined with the social stigma surrounding aids (*sic*) and homosexuality, I spent the next ten years in deep depression waiting for the first purple lesion to appear, the first hacking cough of hundreds to come, the first chill of a flu that never leaves.

For me, the symptoms never arrived. They did, however, afflict ten people whom I loved with all my heart. For a moment, think about losing ten people you love with all your heart, losing nearly

*I refuse to capitalize *hiv* and *aids* because these powerful words scare. Why give them any additional power? Where is the rule that acronyms need to be capitalized? Consider ''cancer'' or ''CANCER.'' Which packs a bigger punch, literally?

a hundred years of combined friendship, shared experience, and love. Is it any wonder I was depressed for ten years?

Travel with me again to another summer, this time in June of 1996. Consider me confident or wacky, but this is my story behind this little book's birth, a story I know that can be called—with a kindly wink—unusual.

I attended a talk by a man whose topic was *forgiving*. With his first words, I was transported to the land of creativity: a book appeared in my mind. Once home, unable to sleep, excited beyond understanding, I called a friend and described in detail the content and layout of the book. If I could have reached into my head, I would have pulled out what you hold in your hand. That is how vivid this creation was and how successful I have been in manifesting this image, an image that continues to grow and change as I grow and change.

I believe on the night I listened to the words about forgiving I was the perfect vessel for Spirit to fill with this vision. At the time, I was unaware of any personal issues revolving around forgiving, therefore receptive. But despite the awesome nature of this happening, the task of plucking the words and pictures I saw in my head did not begin until the following September. Fear kept me locked in uncertainty. Who was *I* to write about forgiveness? I have no degree in psychology or divinity. My writing never centered on nonfiction, much less on a topic as difficult as forgiving. All I have is experience. Apparently, that was all that was required, as Spirit would not let me escape from my assignment. Its pursuit of me was patient, yet relentless.

Finally, one Sunday evening as I was tidying my home, new ideas about the book flooded my mind, but I kept doing, kept cleaning. Without warning, a wave of "electricity," simultaneously warm and chilling, washed through my entire body. It totally debilitated me so that I had to stop in my tracks. The feeling was wondrous and brought a smile to my face. I remember saying that now was as good a time as any, so I thought, "Lord, speak to me. Thy servant is willing to listen." The answer I received was so simple, so distinct, so declarative: "Get busy on the book!" So I did.

Since surrendering to the seed of this extraordinary experience, I have used the forgiving process to become aware of other subjects

I needed to forgive, including myself. It is called "walking my talk."

Sometimes living what I "preach" is not easy. After all, I am human, albeit a spiritual being having a human experience. I am not a guru, a therapist, a professor. No initials of this or that follow my name. I am not a woo-woo fanatic. Like you, I am trying to make sense of this human experience. Like you, I am a student of life, also a teacher. Like you, I search for love, fulfillment, peace.

Perhaps what best qualifies me to have written a book on forgiving is that I know what it is like to feel sad and lonely and purposeless, to believe that life is totally unfair, a miserable chore, some cosmic and humorless joke. Looking at people in the middle of their crap I say to myself, "I know what that's like, and I know life doesn't have to be that way." Contracting hiv forced me to look at my crap, to wade through the illusions of poor self-esteem and death, in order to find the beauty of my individuality and the joys of my purpose. This is why contracting hiv was one of the best events in my life.

Before you dismiss me as being vulgar, the good book *Webster's* defines *crap* as "nonsense, rubbish." And our issues—certainly mine—when thoughtfully examined, many times do contradict good sense and create the garbage that clogs and litters our minds. This is not meant to minimize my or anyone's issues, but these illusions prevent us from experiencing the beauty of life, the beauty of who we really are—a light of love. I wish I could hug people and by some cosmic process of osmosis transfer what I have learned from my heart to the very heart of that person. Since I have not mastered this method—yet—I wrote *The Little Book on Forgiving* instead.

But for ten years I coped with my hiv status as best I could with what few tools I had. In December of 1992, when yet another dear friend passed on, I died. I died emotionally, mentally, spiritually. I became a zombie—eating, breathing, working, the walking dead, numb with grief.

Around Christmas—how perfect—I decided this condition could not continue. I did not know what, how, or where to change this condition, only that it was unacceptable. Bottom line? Dying of aids was a totally unacceptable way of living. I refused the reality that stared back at me in black and white print, that blared forth from the television, that I saw in the faces of my sick friends. In my own way, I started to forgive myself and acquired a new respect and appreciation for my life. I believe this is a major reason why to this day I have yet to manifest any physical signs of hiv. I know that I, the old me, had to die in order to be reborn, to begin anew.

My path of resurrection led me to the Grief Group at the Colorado aids (*sic*) Project, the Experience, a nonprofit organization for self-empowerment, and Science of Mind principles. Through the help and love of many, I found enlightenment and incredible levels of love, peace, and freedom.

Life still challenges me—boy does it ever! I still deal with my hiv and feeling undesirable, unworthy, unclean, because I still give the virus that power. But I am not this virus unless I choose to define myself by the illusion of its disastrous traits. The more I surrender to Spirit, the more I recall my truth, and the more I re-mind myself—think differently—the less power I grant to the virus. On some level, I even love it. Step by step, more peace is mine.

Recently, I was assessing my life so far when a question popped into my head: "What has been the value of hiv and never having had a significant relationship?" The answer came without hesitation: "These two facts brought me closer to God." Suddenly, the value of my issues became invaluable—and their reality-based shape? Transcendent, priceless gifts. I had transformed my gravest life-threatening liabilities into my greatest life-giving assets.

Wisdom comes from asking the right question. A personally resonant answer only produces more questions which beg more answers. Wisdom is the peeled onion unveiling layer after layer of revelation. When I asked the above question, I was referring to a human, lover type of relationship. The next question I asked was, "What about my relationship with God?" I think I got a new onion.

Your path will take you down a different road, but all roads lead to the same destination: change. By remembering your purpose, your birthright and heritage, by embracing the very cause of your pain, and by surrendering to your Spiritual Nature—or whatever you wish to name your life energy—you forgive. You give to yourself for a reason or reasons: to heal, to move on, to discover lost or new joys—whatever reason motivates you. Suddenly, the gift of life is worth expressing, preserving, cherishing. The release of fears and pains from the past lets love and joy fill your consciousness, your present moment. Able to define what peace and freedom look like in your life, you touch others, and they in turn touch others. Spread across the world, this synergy of love neutralizes all the hate and conflict that forces the world to its knees. This is why you and your healing are so very important to our world. But we cannot heal the world without first changing our minds about the world.

The book you hold is not the only way to travel the road toward forgiving, peace, and freedom. It is simply one way.

The Little Book on Forgiving aims at the heart. This is where healing yourself and the world begins. In your heart! Nowhere else.

On behalf of the world, thank you for reading this far. Thank you for making the effort to heal yourself and heal the world.

THINK BIG!
ACHIEVE BIG!

Hatred is not diminished by hatred at any time.
Hatred is diminished by love—
this is the eternal law.

THE DHAMMAPADA

One word frees us of all the weight
and pain of life: That word is love.

SOPHOCLES

What Is Forgiving?

Forgiving Defined

To forgive is an act of love. It is an expression of love for yourself and for the subject you forgive. Forgiving transforms your mind, where you conceive it, and your heart, where you feel it. You begin to forgive when you think your first thought about forgiving. Every single, solitary second is ripe with this potential. You choose which moment to begin, consciously or not. Personal peace and fulfilling freedom are only a thought away, but not without first forgiving.

To forgive means that you surrender all feeling of retaliation, revenge and/or repayment toward the subject that you perceive has hurt you. Forgiving does not include overlooking or justifying a kind of behavior like dishonesty or violence or drinking or drugging. Forgiving does not include absolution for an admitted offense. You may never get such an admission. That is to condone, to excuse, or to pardon, but not to forgive.

To forgive is unconditional. To forgive is an act of courage and empowerment. To forgive is an act of healing—your healing. When you heal, the world heals, and the world is in great need of your efforts.

Start with this mind-boggling premise: You—and you alone—possess the potential to forge a unique declaration of truth on this planet. Try not to shrink from this statement for whatever reason because deep down inside you know that it is true. Stop pretending that you don't. The challenge is to bring that truth into the light of your awareness, until you are able to express your singular truth. Whether you touch one or millions—the number is unimportant—the world will be a better place. You have no idea whom you may affect with your truth. Whether or not you even know if you have touched anyone, the seeds you plant could feed any number of hungry souls anywhere.

And people are hungry! You are hungry! You may be blessed with a full stomach, but something within you feels starved. The sustenance to nourish that feeling you will not find wrapped in plastic in the refrigerator.

Being unwanted, unloved, uncared for, forgotten by everyone; I think that is a much greater hunger, a much greater poverty than the person who has nothing to eat. . . . We must find each other.

MOTHER TERESA

By opening and reading this book you have made a decision. You desire to change. Something is not right in your life. You may not know what it is and are confused. You may know exactly what it is and are still confused. One thing is certain: the status quo of your life is acceptable no more.

Since you chose a book on forgiving—no one chose it for you—someone or something has hurt you. On some level you are ready to forgive.

You definitely desire to forgive because you know exactly who or what hurt you. You know exactly how this hurt manifests in your life. You seek specifically to surrender your pain, your dysfunction, your anger, your apathy. Forgiveness is your way to peace and freedom. All that is missing is the "how to."

You may know merely that something is wrong. This may be an indication of something deeper or that whatever is bothering you is not about you. Yes, hard as it may seem, not everything is about you. Forgiving may or may not be the answer, but you are willing to give this book a shot.

In either case, willingness is essential. In either case, you —and only you—know what you are feeling.

Why do humans forgive? To alleviate the discomfort of distress, inner imbalance, and recurrent, harmful habits. Life can be a juggling act, yet when so many plates crash, a life of magical zest—which is possible—seems impossible. You search for balance, both the inner balance of a peaceful psyche and the outer balance of joyful, day-to-day living. But to locate comfort, you cannot turn your back on your discomforts. In fact, be thankful for them. They are the bricks that pave the road to your greater self-discovery and are therefore blessings of inestimable value. That may not be easy to swallow at this moment, but hold on to this thought throughout the process.

If forgiving is an action you decide to pursue, only you define whether or not you do honestly forgive and surrender your suffering. For some, reading this far is a great success. Others may define their success only after completing this process five times.

How do you know if you have truly forgiven? If you have to ask yourself the question, you have achieved some degree of forgiveness, but you have not completely forgiven. That may be perfectly okay for you, but this is a matter for the heart. And the heart does not lie. Convince your mind that you forgive; the heart will follow. You will know when you *know*, quite likely unexpectedly; but something wonderful suddenly takes the place of something icky, and a wash of warm love and peace flows over you. You literally awake, emotionally replenished, mentally restored, bodily refreshed, spiritually revitalized.

But success or failure is not the question. Keeping your idea of forgiving at the forefront of your mind and expanding your consciousness to live a better way—these are the dares that summon you to a higher calling. There is no failure, only growth forward. The change you seek is up to you. What happens to you and in your life is up to you.

Do not fear mistakes—there are none.

MILES DAVIS

This book is for people who know they have the need to forgive. This book is for people who might have an idea they need to forgive. This book is a process of evaluation and discovery. This book is meant to empower you to take control of your life, to find the love—both the love of others and self-love—that may be missing in your life. When you do this, all sorts of good things happen. You define what those good things are.

Subjects of Forgiving

Forgiveness requires a subject to forgive, which may encompass a combination.

1. Someone hurt you, and you know exactly who this is and what it is about.
2. Someone hurt you, but you are unsure of the identity or vague about the circumstances.
3. Someone from your past hurt you, and this still affects your life today.
4. Someone hurt you and is totally unaware of his or her actions.
5. Someone hurt you and did so purposely.
6. Someone who perceives he or she has hurt you asks for your forgiveness.
7. Some things or groups or a representative hurt you.
8. Someone or something hurt you, and you think this is the Universe, Fate, God.
9. With any of the above scenarios, the person hurt may be someone you love very much.

10. The subject you wish to forgive is yourself.

Do as the heroes have done,
forget your evil;
With them forgive yourself.

SHAKESPEARE, *A Winter's Tale*

Whatever the case, you perceive an injury or wrong perpetrated by a causing force. This perception lives in your mind. Only when you examine your perception do you discover that deeper issues may exist.

Forgiving engages your self-image and the roles you play in life. Feelings of both inferiority and superiority reveal a lack of love and approval and acceptance, making forgiving more agonizing and saddening than the original cause of your pain. The issues at the core of your situation may have more to do with the subject you desire to forgive, but this still affects you personally.

He or she may need to feel superior because of a feeling of inferiority, a lack of self-esteem. No matter how hard you try, you cannot fix or rescue them, you maybe feel guilty because of it, so you take on the role of victim. If you can look at the perceived persecutor behind your pain compassionately, you see this need to be loved not being returned. Maybe *you* are the persecutor and do not like what this role says about you. Guilt in all its guises rears its ugly head.

Understand that the subject you forgive may not necessarily want or need your forgiveness, may never know you have forgiven, may be totally unaware of injuries done to you. If he or she is made aware of injuries, your forgiveness may convey a healing. That is a good thing, but do not let it be the motivation to forgive. The healing is for *you*. Forgiveness is for the one forgiving.

What about the need to forgive the intangible? For example, everyone who hates you; a social or professional group that denied you membership; the President who sent a son to war, or who failed to wage war on a disease causing the deaths of friends; a radical terrorist who bombed the workplace of your spouse; the government that caused the loss of your business; the manufacturers of a defective product that killed a loved one; a bigoted leader whose group targets a group you belong to; a church whose dogma does you damage. *Anger toward the intangible will consume you with frustration.* This big thing is outside of your control.

Whether the subject you desire to forgive is intangible or sleeps next to you, control what you *can* control: what and how you think and feel. It is simplistic to say, "It's all in your mind, change it." That is cruel to say to someone who is in the midst of painful turmoil. But embedded in this cliché lies a rock of truth. In essence, your thoughts and perceptions block your movement forward. Changing your thoughts and perceptions can happen overnight, but *growth* depends on your willingness to change what you control, and that is *thought*.

A lack of self-esteem can be the root cause of what you think you lack control over. The tendency to blame others for one's sorry state of affairs masks your inability to accept yourself as you are. If you see racism in anyone who challenges you because you are black, or homophobia because you are gay, personal guilt may devalue your feelings of self-worth. By blaming the Universe for being black or gay, you pick a fight you cannot win. Besides, you are not your body. You are the power that lives within it.

Playing the persecutor, victim, or rescuer in any situation zaps that power. You short-circuit the source of power you possess at the very time you need it the most. You make decisions that keep you unhappy. You feel unable to break these habits yet know your very own decisions and habits cause your unhappiness. Life becomes a treadmill and not a reason to rejoice.

If you react to situations in the present through the eyes of your past, you are destined to repeat ineffective behavior until you uncover the root cause. Realize that your goal is to look upon your life through the eyes of the present. The past does not change; what you think about it does—and so, you change.

Nothing changes more consistently than the past. The past that influences our lives is not what actually happened but what we believe happened.

GERALD W. JOHNSON

You are not your situations, your story, your facts, or your events, yet how profoundly they affect you! Some happened a day ago, some years ago. Some situations survive hundreds of generations and still affect people today. The Middle East conflict did not begin in 1967, but long before the arrival of Jesus Christ. The strife in Bosnia did not begin in 1990, nor in 1914 as a primary cause of World War I, but before the time of Charlemagne. The racial turmoil in the United States does not stem from the Civil War, but from five hundred years ago when this country was first settled.

> *The holiest of all spots on earth is where an ancient hatred has become a present love.*
>
> A COURSE IN MIRACLES

Whole cultures have not admitted wrongs nor learned to forgive. No one alive may know how a conflict started, but wrongs are committed perpetually, generation after generation. Revenge rules the people. Until societies on a national, continental, and global level ask for and give each other forgiveness, ask for and give members within their own society forgiveness, healing will never occur. Peace and freedom, personal and worldwide, will be usurped by planetary revenge. The cost and loss are staggering.

You are one person. You affect and are affected by the collective consciousness of this planet. This is why when one person forgives, the world heals. This is why when you forgive, you commit an act of love. *You are the world!*

Your Higher Power

How do you forgive when actions toward you personally or toward someone you love have been horrendous, harmful, immoral? You cannot do it alone. And you are *never* alone.

There is a Higher Power within you. Call it God, call it Ra, call it Buddha, call it Henry Hossenfeffer. Call IT whatever you *wish*. IT is the source of your intuition, your inspiration, your imagination. IT is

Lead me from the unreal to the real.
Lead me from darkness to light.
Lead me from death to immortality.

BRIHADARANYAKA UPANISHAD

the source of those sweet, twinkling inklings that bead like a dew-drop in your conscience, that flit like a butterfly within your belly.

While you may change, know that IT never does. IT is the Great Changeless. IT has no beginning and no end. IT is always present, always was, always will be in everyone and everything. How then could IT change, and into what would IT change—for that which IT would change into, IT already is.

Whatever you call IT, know that IT exists within you. IT goes where you go—and beyond.

Even if you are agnostic or atheistic or pantheistic, your power is your Consciousness. Same thing. You decide the name and character of your Higher Power. Choose something that represents your idea of a Higher Power. That may be a stuffed animal, a chair, the 'Energy within My Consciousness,' whatever comforts you. Bad memories from bad experiences as a member of some religion hopefully will not block your ability to believe in a Higher Power. Try not to allow personal history to interfere with you and your Source. Realize that at any given moment you are always doing your best. You decide what would be better, if you are capable of doing better, when you do better.

This Power is not hiding, nor does It lie dormant, nor has It ever forsaken you. Search within. There you find It, there you activate It, there you return to Its succor where It always has been.

How do you do this? By merely thinking about It. By focusing your thoughts on this Presence within you, It will answer your questions, It will guide you, It will comfort you. Pay attention to It, partner It, create with It, love It. It will never desert you. With a thought, you switch It on!

May the Force be with you.

GEORGE LUCAS

When the movie *Star Wars* appeared, a global consciousness was tapped. The story is not just comic-book science fiction. We are all Luke Skywalkers searching for our truth. And the truth Luke found in Obi Wan, Yoda, and his father was no greater than what he discovered in himself.

The same applies to Jesus Christ, Moses, Muhammad or the Buddha. They accessed, focused on, and listened to the same Power that resides within you. Yet no one and no religion monopolizes this Power—not the Mormons, Muslims, Christians, Buddhists, or any New Age sect. The Power is there for you, too.

This book uses words for the Higher Power not to make you uncomfortable, but for the sake of communication. Substitute your own word for what is used. The human race has only put some letters and sounds together to name the Nameless. Suggestions for your Nameless:*

God	Allah	Buddha
Ra	Great Spirit	Universe
The Divine	The Christ Within	Higher Energy
Spirit	I	Mind
Silent Partner	The Presence	Mother Goddess
Force	Nature	Light of Life
Higher Power	Higher Consciousness	Great Love
Greater Self	The Nameless	The Changeless
Phyllis	George	?

*In this book when a name for God is capitalized, the name refers to a God Entity. When the same word is used in lower case, the word refers to a human entity. Examples: Higher Power, higher power; Conscience, your conscience; Love, love of woman.

There are almost six billion people in the world. There are almost six billion ideas of God. Your idea of God is no less valid than Marianne Williamson's or the Dalai Lama's. Find comfort and a partner in the name you give your Nameless.

The only words you can speak and be identified with wisely, are, "I am my own understanding of God."

EMMA CURTIS HOPKINS

They can because they think they can.

VIRGIL

He who has begun his task has half done it.

HORACE

Nothing will come of nothing.

SHAKESPEARE, *King Lear*

Tools

Your Desire
Your Mind
Your Heart
Paper or Notebook
Pen or Pencil
Tape Recorder (optional)
Your Higher Power

You begin with your desire to forgive. There is no other starting point. **Your desire** may be a conscious thought or an unconscious notion. Even if you are not yet sure you want to forgive, a desire within you compels you to act. Otherwise, you would not be reading this sentence.

You do nothing without your **mind and heart**. Bring them and use them consciously. The key word is *consciously*. Be present for this process.

Get a **notebook**, one that you like. Pick a favorite color; lined wide or thin or unlined; 39¢ or leather-bound; pictures and quotations and dates or not; made from scratch paper and what is on

29

hand, an Indian tablet or rich bond. Choose what pleases you.

Get a **pen or pencil** or a selection of pens and pencils. Light or dark lead; dollar packets of ten or drafting-quality; colored inks, black or blue; wide or fine point; fat or thin barrel; a give-away or a hundred dollars. Choose what pleases you.

A **tape recorder** is optional. If you cannot or do not like to write, record your thoughts orally. A large reel-to-reel with microphone or pocket-sized. Choose what pleases you.

Your Higher Power is not a requirement, but it is not an option either. It is a given. It goes where you go. It *is* you. It is the energy of your existence. Call It whatever you wish. Call upon It whenever you wish. Think of It as your Tutor. It is the Greatest Learning Partner you have.

> *How many ideas go unexplored because*
> *people lack the courage to fail?*
>
> WILBUR M. MC FEELY

Actions

Prayer
Exercises
Affirmations
In Silence
My Declaration to Forgive

These Actions follow each Step. They are suggestions. Some of them will make you uncomfortable or make you laugh; some of them will induce revelation, some a snore. They are to help you, not hinder you. Do what you want to do.

A **Prayer** begins the Action portion of each step. In prayer you speak to your Higher Power, you address It with earnest requests. If the word or action of "prayer" is uncomfortable for you, think of it as speaking to yourself.

The **Exercises** provide exploration. Use your notebook. Use a computer if you like; however, a connection links your thought with the physical act of writing, and unedited action reveals truth. Purge, uncover, flow with your thoughts. Silence your judgment.

This is not English 101 (nor is it Speech 101 if you use a recorder). You are the ultimate evaluator.

An **Affirmation** is a statement of fact, a validation, a confirmation, an assertion, a decree, a testament. State your affirmations positively, with as much conviction as you have in the moment. Assert your truth as your reality now. Not soon, not tomorrow, not next year. *Now!* In this second! At this moment! An affirmation is not passive; it is an action of your mind. An affirmation taps the power of your consciousness to co-create what you desire in your reality.

In Silence poses questions or ideas for meditation. In this state, listen to your Higher Power. If you are unfamiliar with the process, simply get comfortable in a quiet room, breathe and relax, clear your mind of its business, and focus on the question. If you have problems with mind chatter, gently tell your ego to please be quiet, you will get back to it later. Let what comes come. If you are familiar with meditating, use whatever process you wish. Record your observations.

My Declaration to Forgive is exactly that. It will expand as you expand. Think of it as an unbreakable contract. Your declaration begins by acknowledging your Higher Power, aligning yourself with It, stating you forgive, accepting peace and freedom, thanking your Higher Power, and surrendering your declaration to It.

As with anything, you get out of this process what you put into it. You get what you desire. If you do not get what you desire, work until you do. Better yet, play until you get what you desire. Make your life your chief recreation, the refreshment of your spirit. Re-create what existed at your birth and exists today: the perfect you.

> *Life shrinks or expands*
> *in proportion to one's courage*
>
> ANAÏS NIN

Steps to Forgiving

*W*hen you decide to forgive,
you open the door
of endless possibility
to peace and freedom.

◆

*All growth is a leap in the dark,
a spontaneous unpremeditated
act without benefit of experience.*

HENRY MILLER

Resistance is the first step to change.

LOUISE HAY

1

Decide to Forgive

You planted a seed to forgive before you picked up this book. Now you are nurturing your seed and willing to give direction to your nurturing. You are actively doing something, maybe small, maybe grand, but you are *acting*. When you decide to forgive, you begin the conscious participation of your achievement. You can begin no other place.

You choose when, how, who, or what it is you forgive. As simple as that seems, be aware, be present and be conscious when you make your choices. Harness your imagination, and answer the question, ''What do I really desire?'' Peace and freedom? First, decide that you desire peace and freedom, then imagine what that looks like to you.

Choices are not made *for* you, but *by* you. If you claim so-and-so made a decision for you, you *chose* to let so-and-so make that decision for you. If you are lonely and friendless because you are nasty, sullen, or shy, you *chose* to behave unfriendly. If you are un-

We cannot live a choiceless life. Every day, every moment, every second there is choice. If it were not so, we would not be individuals.

ERNEST HOLMES

employed because you fail to perform your job, you *chose* not to do your job. If your lover treats you like a doormat, you *chose* to be walked and wiped upon. If you are a miserable millionaire, you *chose* misery in the midst of plenty. The consequences of your choices are a logical progression of your thoughts and behaviors.

Upbringing, genes, and traits—physical, mental, and emotional—impact who you are, but your life is mostly a result of choices you made. Your decisions have had consequences. If you do not like your present situation, make *new* choices and *new* decisions that yield your desired consequences. Recognize your responsibility for what your life looks like, and the exciting potential you possess.

That seed to forgive which you planted in the past sprouts in the present to bear fruit in the future, of a nature as yet unknown. Already you have made new choices. You decided that your present circumstances are no longer acceptable. Your pain, your misery, your ambivalence, your grumpiness, your depression—all are no longer acceptable.

At this point, you have *decided* forgiveness is an issue for you. You decided to pick up this book. The title is obvious. You know what it is about. If you are reading this sentence, you *decided* the book was worth investigating. You will decide if you want to continue reading or put the book down and watch television, play ball, or go shopping. If you continue this process, you may—*at any point*—change your mind. That is important to realize. You may change your decision at any given moment. Take responsibility for the consequences that follow.

After making a decision, make a commitment. If you feel you cannot do this right now, you have made another decision. Do not judge yourself as inadequate, cowardly, or weak. You will be ready when you are ready.

Be wary of self-sabotage. Admitting defeat, finding distraction, accepting the opinions of others—any and all can prevent you from moving forward. Keep a vigilant watch on forces that sabotage your decision to forgive. They are sneaky. Trust can be a big issue: trusting yourself, trusting a process, trusting your Higher Power. At times, the known is more acceptable than the unknown because there is a payoff when you do not explore the causes of your problems: you do not have to face your fears. Like a warm blanket, fear wraps you in deceptive comfort and prevents you from seeing the larger payoffs life has to offer.

A decision *not* to commit to forgiving does not exclude gathering information. You achieve solutions by exploration. This is how you form a decision that you are comfortable with and commit to it. This is how you evolve.

> *Do what you fear to do,*
> *and the death of fear is certain.*
>
> RALPH WALDO EMERSON

You are exploring forgiving to find comfort in your life, a personal kind of peace and freedom. Expect discomfort along the path. The discomfort you feel in your present life leads you to desire change. At any point in this process, you decide which is more tolerable. What are you willing to tolerate? What are you willing to change? Be resolute and keep your eye on the goal of peace and freedom. Anything else is an obstruction.

Forgiving is a road either rocky or smooth. At every juncture, you choose which road you take. Your journey will be as easy— or as hard—as you decide to make it. If you think it is going to be hard, then it will be hard. Think your travels easy, they will be. It is your call. Only you know if you are deluding yourself.

You may start this book twenty-two times before you finally complete it, or you may skim several steps and complete the process in hours. You decide when you have completed the process, but you cannot begin the process at step five. You begin when you decide to forgive.

Above all else, through the process that lies ahead, show yourself compassion. You deserve it. You will need it. So be, be, be compassionate to yourself! Gentle and loving as well.

Also, be an active agent, a co-creator along with your Higher Power, to manifest your desired outcome, which is peace and freedom. You hold the ball of your life. It is in your court. Take the ball and run with it! Anything else is like watching your life from the sidelines.

The person who does not make a choice makes a choice.

JEWISH PROVERB

Prayer   Use this or write your own.

> Dear Spirit,
> I am so sad, so miserable.
> I have been betrayed.
> I hurt and I cannot rid myself of this hurt.
> Please help me.
> Please cleanse me of this pain.
> Please show me the Light.
> Please show me *my* Light.
> Please show me the Light in my betrayer.
> Release me from my self-inflicted bondage that I
>   may express my freedom.
> Release me from my unnatural turmoil that I may
>   feel my inborn peace.
> Please show me the Light of forgiveness.
> Thank you. Thank you. Thank you.
> Amen.

Exercises   Answer any of these questions and statements in your notebook. If anything else comes to mind, write about that.

1. What does forgiveness mean to me?
2. Whom or what do I need to forgive? Why do I need to forgive this subject?

Self	Bosses	The President
Parents	Lawyers	The Pope
Spouse	Doctors	My Country
Children	Teachers	A Race, Nationality
Siblings	Managers	A Group of People
A Relative	Accountants	A Club or Institution

3. How do I sabotage myself? What do I not trust?
4. What decisions do I desire to commit to?
5. What do peace and freedom look like to me?
6. How would I like to play at making my life my chief recreation? What perfection existed at my birth, that I would like to re-create now?
7. What is my payoff when I do not face my fears?

Affirmations

Use these suggestions or write your own in your notebook. Choose words that are positive. For example, do not say, "My pain is gone." That acknowledges pain. Say, "My health appears." Fill in the blanks with the subject you desire to forgive. Believe your affirmation the moment you say it.

1. I forgive you _____. My forgiveness is complete.
2. I affirm that I forgive_____. I affirm that I forgive _____ right now. I affirm that I forgive _____ with my whole heart.
3. I proclaim that the veil of mystery disappears. It disappears at this very moment. Understanding, knowledge, and clear thinking arise in my mind as I think this thought. I trust myself. I trust my Higher Power. I proclaim that peace and freedom are mine now.

In Silence Find a quiet space, indoors or outdoors. Take a few deep breaths. Relax your body. Quiet your mind. Ask any of these questions or visualize any of the suggestions. Ask your own questions, create your own visualizations. Listen for the answers. Later, record any observations you choose.

1. What is bothering me? Why am I so upset? Please help me.
2. Whom or what do I need to forgive?
3. I look for my Higher Power. I find my Higher Power. Speak to me. I am ready to listen.
4. I close my eyes and my imagination soars. I see what peace and freedom look like for me.
5. Your mind is full of ego chatter. Tell your ego to be quiet, that you love it, that you are not leaving it behind on this journey. Tell your ego to come along with you, but that you are moving on and moving forward. Be gently and lovingly insistent.

My Declaration to Forgive

As always, invoke your word for your Higher Power. Fill in the blank with the subject you have decided to forgive. The Declaration expands with each step. If you wish to change what is used, relate your changes to the step you experience. Make your changes positive. Thank your Higher Power for anything you choose. Write out your Declaration, record it, say it, think it—as often as you desire.

> Divine Being,
> With this thought I align myself with You.
> I know Your Power is the power within me.
> I declare right here and now
> that I forgive _____.
> Peace and Freedom are mine.
> I thank myself for my decision.
> I thank You for my decision.
> Amen.

Releasing your desires and unleashing
your Higher Power are ultimate acts of
faith in your Higher Power
—and in yourself.

◆

*This is the other gold, that glows in your chest
when you love.*

RUMI

That is perfect.
This is perfect.
Take perfect from perfect,
                    the remainder is perfect.

THE UPANISHADS

2

Let Go and Set Loose

You have made some decisions about forgiving. They may be explicit, and you are very clear about your situation. They may be vague, and you are still exploring the realm of forgiving. Instead of receiving answers, more questions arise. No matter where you find yourself in this process of forgiving, you may wonder why you started it. What now?

In either case, what do you do with these decisions you have made? What do you do with this bag you are left holding?

Give it up. It is as simple and sane as that. Just when you get started, give up your decisions to your Higher Power. Access It, use It. Get your decisions out of your head and into the Cosmos.

Say: "At this moment, H. P., I'm done with this issue. I'm

turning it over to You. It's Yours now. Take it. Make it happen. I've made my decision. I've spoken my word. I set loose my power and Your Power to make my decision my reality.''

Although you give your problem to your Source, your Source does not now "have" the problem. Problems are not recognizable concepts to the Source. You are still the one with the problem. Your intention is to find assistance in order to find a solution. Your Source is always ready to assist you and has oodles of solutions to reveal to you.

But in your silence or meditations is *not* where you *solve* the problem. Use this time to listen to your Source. *Let come what comes.* Whether that be verbal messages, pictures, sensations, inklings— trust yourself to understand the information if not immediately, then later. Get quiet and you get clear. Once you align yourself with your Source, you reveal the solutions to yourself.

When you let go and set loose, believe that the statements you make are so. Believe they are realized in your life. At that moment, that is how you feel. If five minutes later or at any time doubt, discomfort, or guilt returns, reaffirm your word. Realize you are changing your thinking.

Old habits of thought can be stubborn and clutching. They may not leave without a fight. This is why reaffirming your word as often as you choose creates new thought patterns. Like a dirt road in a farm field that disappears from lack of use, so do your old habits disappear when you stop thinking them. Replace the old beliefs with new beliefs. *Believe* in the certitude that what you desire manifests. *Believe* that your Source works with unshakable constancy. Dump the doubt! It's useless.

Try not to force your declaration. Let it flow out of you with perfect confidence. Simply let it be. Act as though the outcome is a given. Think only thoughts of achievement. Your Higher Power takes care of the details, but let It know you desire Its help and with what.

Letting go is the ultimate act of faith in your Higher Power. It is also the ultimate act of faith in yourself. The two are inseparable because you are one and the same. You are *a part* of the Cosmos, not *apart* from the Cosmos. The same Force that created and is the Cosmos created and is in you. It can handle your problems. Trust It, trust yourself. Transcend the impossible and the invisible. Believe in the possible and the visible.

'he only real faith is blind faith.

ANONYMOUS

When you set loose your Higher Power, you free the power that already exists within you, you plug into your Higher Power. You connect with your Higher Power, then disconnect with this world, in order to reconnect with your Higher Power. *Connect, disconnect, reconnect.* When you reconnect with this world, it is different. Your consciousness about truth and reality shifts. You set loose power, your own internal power and the Power of the Universe.

If you keep yourself in a state of anger and frustration and depression and apathy, your vital energy remains a closed conduit. Releasing your desires and unleashing your energy become impossible. Negative thoughts clog your very own personal pipeline to the Source of All. Positive thoughts flush out this pipeline, and the flow of your energy reaches the Cosmic Dynamo.

A rock of plutonium radiates energy, but until its internal properties are properly accessed, it remains a glob of potential. Only when its internal properties are accessed does it exhibit the colossal manifestation of powering cities and societies.

You are like a ball of plutonium. You radiate energy. If you never access your energy, you *still* radiate energy. Only when you access your internal energy will you exhibit the colossal manifestation of powering your life.

And you drive your own life! Life does not drive you. You alone give it a course to travel. But if you become lost, know that a Passenger hitchhikes with you wherever you go. Ask It for direction, but know your destination.

What if you do not know where you want to go? What if all this talk about forgiving and Higher Power makes a muddle of your mind? What if all this is just a bunch of bunk?

Again, you choose what you believe, what you accept. Whatever that looks like to you is perfect for you. Much of what you do depends on your expectations. Expect to forgive without doubt, with passionate certitude, and you will. *You do.* Expect miracles with total conviction.

A perceived failure can sabotage your progress. A skeptic may require a miracle and, when one does not appear, may abandon any process of forgiving, not understanding that skepticism blocks any chance that a miracle shall occur. Expecting peace and freedom without confronting issues that obstruct and thwart obtaining peace and freedom forecasts only self-defeat. Forgiving remains unattainable.

What are you willing to change? Answer that and you decide your next action. Either you continue this process—or any process—and you grow and evolve, or you discontinue this process. Growth and evolution come when and how you decide to grow and evolve.

Truly releasing your decision to forgive brings a sigh of relief, lightens a burden on your shoulders. Truly unleashing your power brings confidence and empowerment, an assurance that your decision to forgive is now your truth, your reality, and a license to utilize your power whenever you wish.

Whether fog enshrouds the port of peace and freedom where you desire to anchor yourself, or you float toward it under clear skies, you cannot fail with such a Wind behind your sails. Only *you* define defeat. Your Partner does not even know the meaning of the word. Your Partner is invincible. And so are *you*.

Miracles are your birthright.
This is what your hope tells you,
and your hope is correct.

EMMA CURTIS HOPKINS

Prayer   Use this or write your own.

Dear Spirit,
I have decided to forgive _____.
Please guide me through the upcoming days and nights.
Light my path
That I might see more clearly.
I'm still unsure about my decision.
I'm still afraid about what is to come.
I'm still feeling the anguish.
I seek to let go of my uncertainty.
I seek to let go of my fears.
I seek to let go of my hurt.
Please take this darkness from me.
Please give me Your Light
That I may see my light, that I may see the light of

_____.

Please set loose Your Power that I may set loose my
   power.
Amen.

Exercises   Answer any of these questions and statements in your notebook. If anything else comes to mind, write about that.

1. What do I long to let go of? What does that feel like to me? When I let go, what do I think I set loose?
2. How do I interpret *connecting, disconnecting,* and *reconnecting*?
3. What are my expectations regarding this process of forgiving? How am I invincible?

Affirmations Use these suggestions or write your own in your notebook.

1. I let go of my decision to forgive
   _____. I set loose my Higher Power. It is so.

2. I affirm that I release my desire to forgive
   _____. I hand over my desire to forgive _____ to my Higher Power. I know this thought makes it happen. I know my Higher Power makes it happen, right now.

3. I affirm that I forgive _____ with my whole heart. My confidence in myself and my Higher Power is solid and true. New thoughts arrive and transform me. I receive love freely and willingly. I give love freely and willingly. Right now, I think only loving thoughts. All is right with me. All

is right with the world. All is right with

_____.

4. I proclaim that all that lives in my mind is thoughts and feelings of joy and happiness, peace and freedom. I further avow that these thoughts set loose my power to direct my life the way I desire. My confidence in myself and my Higher Power is solid and true. I state that this is so at this very moment.
5. At this very moment, I declare that I find and know and feel the flow of Life. My thoughts flow freely. I let go and set loose my power.

In Silence Find your quiet. Use these suggestions. Ask or envision anything you choose. Record any observations.

1. I look into my heart. There I find love for

   _____.

2. I sense the Power I set loose. Reveal Yourself to me.

3. I ask for guidance. As the veil of confusion draws back, all I feel is goodness and truth. I am ready to listen.

My Declaration to Forgive

Add the italicized statements. Add or change anything you desire.
Make your changes positive.

> O Light of Life,
> With this thought I align myself with You.
> I know Your Power is the power within me.
> I declare right here and now
> that I forgive _____.
> *I release my capacity to love _____.*
> Peace and Freedom are mine.
> *Thank You for helping me.*
> *I let go of this declaration and set*
> *loose the Power of the Universe.*
> Amen.

*K*now your emotions.
Those that keep you from
peace and freedom—dump!

◆

*And ye shall know the truth,
and the truth shall set you free.*

JOHN 8:32

*The truth will set you free.
But first, it will make you angry.*

ANONYMOUS

3

Clarify Your Feelings

Before deciding to forgive, you felt a certain way about your life, about yourself, about the person you aspire to forgive. Your feelings may be definite. If not, even confusion or indifference is a way of feeling. In either case, what meaning does this mass of emotion hold for you? Fine-tuning what you feel bestows clarification, comprehension, and occasion for growth.

Too often, you may define yourself by situations surrounding you. Seek the center within. Situations are outside of you. Though you have chosen to be the center of an exterior situation, make a different choice. Ask your heart for guidance. Define yourself by that and good will follow.

Bad things happen. Without notice, life can tumble down about you causing spiritual, financial, emotional, physical, or mental ruin. Your life seems ugly, unwanted, expressing an exaggerated fragility incapable of withstanding the onslaught heaved upon it. You appear helpless, painfully vulnerable. Contemplating life with greater purpose becomes an effort in futility, yet many times this is when true contemplation begins and greater purpose is found. Be grateful for this time as you search "to make sense of it all."

Know that you are not your exterior situations. Know that you are not helpless, that the appearance is fake and false. Know that vulnerability need not be painful, but joyful, for this is when your heart and mind are open to receive answers. Know that your interior center is not brittle, feeble or impotent, but secure, resilient and valorous. The essence of your life contains strength beyond human measure. Command it!

How you recover from misfortune, shock, hurt, or harm reflects in direct proportion how deeply you embrace your life force. In the past, you may have met great challenge with great result. You utilized religious or psychological knowledge and language, common sense, or achieved by chance. What is not working for you now? What is no longer—or never was—solid in what you think about life? What feelings prevent you from embracing life?

You never know when or where a nugget of truth will reveal itself. Be conscious of where you are, what you are doing, what is happening around you. This is your life that you are experiencing! For Heaven's sake—no, for *your* sake!—pay attention. Be open to possibility.

You discover a thousand different ways: meditating, thinking, journaling; swimming in the sea, hiking in the mountains; fishing, golfing, shopping; talking to someone, talking to yourself, talking to your dog, cat, bird, fish, ferret; talking to the stars, moon, sun, grass, trees, flowers; reading, listening to music, watching a movie, a concert, a sunrise, a sunset, a baseball game; in a class, in the shower, in the car, in the garden, in the gym; cooking, cleaning, bathing a baby, tending a wound, tying a tie, changing the oil; at work, at play, asleep. Or just by being.

Rarely do you discover anything while sitting in front of the

Anywhere is the center of the earth.

BLACK ELK

television except that there is yet another new deodorant that will save your life and that it is time for bed. News Flash! A deodorant will never save your life; and the time that has passed is lost to you forever.

What do you do with your time when you wait? Curse, grumble, fidget, work yourself into a state of anger and frustration? These times can be gifts of pause. They can be serendipitous because of the blessing they bring to your busy or boring day. They are moments of possibility, a chance for your brain to quiet. What rises in your consciousness is the blessing. You may do a lot of waiting in lines at the bank, the grocery store, ticket outlets, the doctor's office. Ever get stuck in traffic? Instead of turning purple with road rage and repeating epithets of a driver's lineage, use this valuable time to turn inward and breathe and repeat your affirmations, your Declaration. Use these snippets of opportunity to clarify your feelings. Use the pause to simply *be*. The potential lying in wait is grand!

Being open means you live your life in a perpetual state of unguardedness and preparedness. Your consciousness is open for business—the business of life. Because you are available, you are ready to receive messages and information no matter where you are or what you are doing. Knowledge, reasons, epiphanies, miracles, the wonder and joy of small things suddenly surface. They surface, not because they were not there. They were always there. Your field of vision rises up and out of the muck and mire on which you chose to focus, and it is *you* who actually surface.

Another veil whisks away its shroud of ignorance to divulge awareness. Another piece of the puzzle slides into place to reveal a more complete picture. If you do not tune your brainwaves of receptivity—your thinking—all you get is static. Nothing can get in, and what is jamming your receptivity cannot get out. All you hear is the annoying, static-like noise of mind chatter, imaginary conversations with people you tell off with matchless skill, or arguments with yourself you cannot win.

Finding the fine line between ana- lyzing and over-analyzing, paying attention to what you are doing, be- ing open to the life that surrounds

We do without doing and everything gets done.

DONALD BLUME

you, simply being in the moment and enjoying it—these are times to know what you feel. You will know when you know; but first you must make the effort to know.

Once you clarify your feelings, acknowledge them, give them their due. Do not be hard on yourself for the feelings you have. They are your feelings. They are valid, no matter what anyone says. Whether you admit it or not, you worked hard for your feelings. You will discard them when they no longer serve your purpose, but until then, *do not* ignore your feelings. Within them lies valuable insight for you to further your awareness.

Whatever painful emotions you have surrounding your desire to forgive may be entirely justified. Cruelty exists. If you are the victim of cruelty, decide how long you want to play the victim. Justification or being right is a poor substitute for peace of mind. Being right is nothing but being right.

Say to yourself or out loud or scream at the top of your lungs, "I'm right, I'm right, I'm right!" Then ask yourself, *"But so what? Where is being right getting me?"* If you answer, "Nowhere," then you are ready to move on. If you cannot answer that question, you are not ready to let go of your justification.

Being right can hold you with a tenacious, strangling grip that is deviously *comfortable!* Change can be more frightening and intimidating than the familiar, and forgiving more excruciating than the event that forced it. If all else is wrong with your world, it is nice to be right about something. However, in this case you stunt your personal growth and do yourself a grave disservice.

You hurt—and if you do not feel your feelings, express them, know them, they will live within you, buried deep and festering, thickly coated by an unwillingness to face them, yet affecting everything you do. Feel your feelings as long as you want, as deeply as you want. Realize, though, that the longer you feel them, the more stuck you will stay until you say, "Enough! I want to move on!" Then, the door to forgiving flings open.

> *Perhaps everything that frightens us is,*
> *in its deepest sense, something helpless*
> *that wants our love.*
>
> RAINER MARIA RILKE

Prayer   Use this or write your own.

> O Great Love,
> Since trying to forgive _____,
> I am a jumble of emotions.
> Sometimes I am angry and lash out.
> Sometimes I am sullen and quiet.
> Sometimes I just don't care about anything.
> Sometimes I feel like I am making great progress,
> And then I feel happiness.
> But something happens and I am brought down again.
> I feel like a slave to my feelings
> Because *they* control *me*,
> Because *I* do not control *them*.
> Sometimes I do not know what I feel or feel nothing
> And wish this would just go away.
> I am here, but I feel starved.
> I hunger for answers, discovery, and revelation.
> I hunger for love and joy and peace of mind.

I hunger to bring love and joy to others.
I hunger to be open to every moment.
Please help me find the sustenance for my soul.
Guide me, govern me, guard me.
Amen.

Exercises Answer any of these questions and statements in your notebook. If anything else comes to mind, write about that.

1. When I think of forgiving_____ how do I feel? Is this different from how I want to feel?
2. What is different from having an emotion and feeling it? What emotions am I reluctant to feel?
3. What obstructions do I want to clarify? Do I want to let these clots go? Why? Why not?
4. When I find myself waiting, I will put the time to good use. I will do the following: _____
   _____.
5. What messages do my feelings have for me?

Affirmations Use these suggestions or write your own in your notebook.

1. I affirm right here and now that my truth comes forward, that I know my truth, that I express my truth. I am aware.
2. I assert my willingness to feel what I feel.
3. I announce to Everything, Everywhere, that I forgive _____.
   All I feel toward _____ is love.
   This is my truth in this moment.

In Silence Find your quiet. Use these suggestions. Ask or envision anything you choose. Record any observations.

1. I am now in touch with my Higher Power. My true feelings reveal themselves.
2. I ask my feelings what messages they have for me.
3. In my mind I see what happens when I forgive

_____.

My Declaration to Forgive

Add the italicized statements. Fill in the blank with your feelings. Use only positive words. If you do not feel anything positive, stop at ''My heart fills with warmth.'' Add or change anything you desire. Make your changes positive.

Dear Nature of Life,
With this thought I align myself with You.
I know Your Power is the power within me.
I declare right here and now
that I forgive _____.
I release my capacity to love _____.
At this very moment, I feel relief. My mind, body, and
emotions relax. My heart fills with warmth, and I feel _____

_____.

Peace and Freedom are mine.
Thank You for my clarity.
I let go of this declaration and set
loose the Power of the Universe.
Amen.

Search for the good. What happens? You find love in all its many wondrous guises!

◆

Look, and you will find it—
what is unsought will go undetected.

SOPHOCLES

In a dark time, the eye begins to see.

THEODORE ROETHKE

4

Look at the Good

Good lives in any situation. *Any situation!* Good lives in any individual. *Any individual!* Good lives in *you*.

How do you find the good? To see it, to know it, to feel it, first you must look for it. You must train your eye to focus on only what is good. If you habitually look for bad, bad is all you see. Break the habit by choosing carefully and consciously what you want to see. Instill a new thinking pattern of seeing only the good in your mind.

What is good about betrayal? What is good about lying and cheating? What is good about abuse—mental, emotional, or physical? What is good about divorce? What is good about aids? What is good about the loss of a limb or mobility or sight? What is good about poverty, murder, theft? What is good about a plane crash that claims the lives of hundreds? What is good about war, the Holocaust, a terrorist bombing? What is good about mental illness? What is good about hunger, homelessness, racism, or abortion? What is good about the death of a child? What is good about death, *period*? What is good about vanity, jealousy, vengeance, loneliness, humiliation, conceit, hostility, guilt, grief, condemnation, helplessness, despondency?

Through challenge you grow, you evolve. You discover strengths you would not ordinarily know existed within yourself, the people you love, complete strangers. You learn compassion for your fellow-humans. You learn to appreciate the good in your life. You learn what is of value to you, what you desire to spend your time on during the moments of your life. You experience the human condition which is your reality on this planet. Therein lies the glory of *being* human. Therein lies the good.

Forgiving provides you with only one of the many challenges you face as a human being. In the experience you bring to the table, you search for meaning. Something hurtful or harmful has happened. You gather information and knowledge in order to understand why this or that happened. You search for purpose, but get out of your own way so you can find it.

And what is your purpose? Joy, harmony, wisdom, creativity. Simple, isn't it? Now that you know your purpose on this planet, you search for these qualities and manifestations in your life earnestly. But most of all, you search for love—to give it and to receive it. Love is your greatest purpose of all. And at its deepest core, forgiving is about love—the basic love for another human and the basic love for yourself.

Love is the central flame of the universe.

ERNEST HOLMES

Like it or not, you were born human. You cannot change this basic fact of your birth and existence. Face it. Being human is weird. Here you are in some fleshy shell having conscious thoughts about whatever. Who has not felt trapped? Whose soul has not yearned to escape, to flee, to fly and soar? And yet, who has not trembled with fear at the thought of leaving this comfortable, fleshy shell? Whose soul has not yearned simply to be left alone?

In any case, you are sharing your experience as a man or woman with almost six billion others. If you are having problems with this experience, why assume the other 5,999,999,999 (give or take a few million) are *not* having problems with this experience? We are in this together. We are all searching for love. *All of us.*

Asking why this person treated me so rotten translates to *why did this person not love me?* Asking why I cannot forgive this person translates to *why can I not love him or her?* Asking why I cannot forgive myself translates to *why do I not love myself?* Consider that the subject you desire to forgive, even if that includes yourself, really cries out for love.

Through the process of forgiving you learn to love again—or rather, you RE-learn to love. You re-learn to love yourself and you re-learn to love others. Forgiving is for the one forgiving. You are *giving for* a reason—to yourself and to others—and that reason always returns to your quest for self-love and your innate desire to bestow your love upon others. What follows naturally is your desire to *be* loved.

Forgiving is a way to focus your eye on the good in yourself and the good in others. It is a way to end a search for love. It is a way to give love. And when you give love, you cannot help but receive love.

In your search for the good, you get back to the basics. You were born out of Love, because of Love, and *as* Love; but you have forgotten the reason for the life you have. You have forgotten your birthright, your heritage, your first lesson. *Now you are remembering.*

Your life may seem like a class in session. It may seem like you have been sent to the dunce's corner or that you are having to repeat over and over a certain scenario until you pass some imaginary test. *Test?* What test? No one ever told you there was a test? If you had been told, you would have paid attention, you would have studied, right?

Something in your life leads you to pay attention *now*, to study *now*, to make the effort *now*. Effort is very important, for without it you stay stuck. Choose consciously on what you decide to focus. Without your participation, life happens to you willy-nilly and you do not make life happen the way you desire.

Do not worry. No matter what comes, you will pass this class of life with flying colors because there is no failure in the class of life! There is no test! There is only evolution, movement forward, a greater awakening of your self-realized truth. The dunce's corner is in your mind. Lock the door to that room, throw away the key, and decide to walk through the always open door of hope.

Consider Anne Frank, Helen Keller, Christopher Reeve. Despite outwardly inhuman challenges and conditions, they all found their good embedded in, because of, and in spite of their challenges and conditions. They looked inward. They changed their thinking, and their realizations guided them to become beacons of love, direction, and enlightenment. They consciously chose to find the good. They decided that good existed in their lives and the lives of others. Each could have elected to remain locked within their bodies and their situations, blaming a nationality, fate, God, bad luck, bad genes, a bad horse. If they had, the world would not be a better place. But lucky for us, they found their good, they found their mission. And then what did they do? *They gave it away. They gave it to us.*

Once you find your good, give it to yourself. Then give your good to the world. Because when you forgive, when you commit an act of love, when you search for and find the good in your life, the world is a better place. Your consciousness shifts; and as it shifts, so does the consciousness of the world.

As a result of betrayal and pain and tragedy, the opportunity is ripe to discern what is of value to you, to set boundaries or expand them where needed. You can discover self-worth, self-reliance, self-love, independence of thought, courage. Challenge allows brilliant ideas to blossom, creates catalysts for creativity, provides direction to your life, and as it does, good is there not only for you personally but for those whom you touch. You inspire others, and they in turn inspire others. The consequences of your decisions extend beyond your backyard. We are all in this together!

Consider life as a mirror, a reflection of your experience. See bad in others, others see bad in you. See their good, others see your good. Withhold your love and cling to your fears, love is withheld from you and your fears fester. Release your love and your fears, others release you, love you, and your fears die. Do not forgive, you are not forgiven. Forgive, you are forgiven.

So where is the love and good admist all your anguish? *That* you must choose and decide, discover on your own, and answer on your own. No crib sheets or cheating allowed. But the good is there! You can find it! Move your focus one degree to the left. Where once you saw only black rock, you now see, shining brightly and gloriously, the precious gems of your goodness, the goodness of others, the goodness of your experience, and the diamond of love.

> *The real voyage of discovery consists not in seeking*
> *new landscapes, but in having new eyes.*
>
> MARCEL PROUST

Prayer Use this or write your own.

To My Higher Good:
You know what is in my heart.
You know that I hurt.
With my whole heart I long to change.
But when I think about my sitution, I see only pain.
When I think about _____, I see only the
   cause of my pain.
Help me think about only the good.
Help me to see the good in my situation.
Help me to see the good in _____.
I know the good is there.
I know that love surrounds me.
Point me in the right direction.
I live in joyous anticipation of this revelation.
Thank you for Your Help.
Amen.

Exercises Answer any of these questions and statements in your notebook. If anything else comes to mind, write about that.

1. What is good about the subject you have decided to forgive? Find the good in a bad situation. Why am I not my situation?
2. What efforts am I making to change my thinking patterns? To forgive? What other areas of my life am I willing to make efforts to change?
3. Write a letter to the subject of your forgiveness—the person, institution, the disease. Tell exactly how you have been hurt by the subject. Close the letter with telling the subject what is good about itself and thank it for the good it gives you.
4. What do I need to re-learn about love?

Affirmations   Write your own or use these suggestions.

1. At this very moment, I see only the good in
   _____. I see only good between us.
   The forgiveness I feel toward_____
   is good.
2. Today, I know and express my goodness. I
   witness only the goodness in others and in
   every situation I encounter. My Higher
   Power guides me and opens my eyes to the
   good. Today, I am rich beyond the world's
   measure for goodness is my treasure all day.
3. Right now, I forgive   _____.
   My efforts to see his/her/its goodness bring
   goodness to me. I return this goodness in all
   I do today, to all I see today. I focus only on
   love today. The value of my life is revealed
   with every breath I take, starting right now.

In Silence Find your quiet. Use these suggestions. Ask or envision anything you choose. Record any observations.

1. With this breath, I believe my life is good. And with this breath, I believe my life is good. And with this breath . . . etc. (Continue as long as you wish.)
2. In your mind, see a small spot of light. It is Love. It gradually grows brighter and larger until it encompasses your entire vision. Ask Your Love what message It has for you.
3. Picture a black rock. Picture it splitting open. Knowing the treasure you find is all yours, what is revealed?
4. Picture the subject you have decided to forgive. Ask what your subject is afraid of. Find your subject's goodness. Ask how you can help him/her/it overcome this fear.

My Declaration to Forgive

Add the italicized statements. If your feelings have changed, change what you stated in the last step. Fill in the last blank with the subject you forgive. Add or change anything you desire. Make your changes positive.

One Mind,
With this thought I align myself with You.
I know Your Power is the power within me.
I declare right here and now that I forgive _____.
I release my capacity to love _____.
At this very moment, I feel relief. My mind, body, and emotions relax. My heart fills with warmth, and I feel _____

_____.
I find and know the good of this experience.
I feel compassion toward _____.
Peace and Freedom are mine.
Thank You for the good in myself and the good in my experience.
I let go of this declaration and set loose the Power of the Universe.
Amen.

*K*now your truth, which is that
you are love. Accept it, then
believe it. The same
truth lives in everyone.

◆

Things do not change: We change.

HENRY DAVID THOREAU

*Healing occurs in the present, not the
past. We are not held back by the love
we didn't receive in the past, but by the
love we're not extending in the present.*

MARIANNE WILLIAMSON

Steps to Forgiving

5

Believe Differently

You possess a wondrous and marvelous ability. You use it thousands of times every day of your life, consciously and unconciously. It gives you the direction of your life. It is what determines how you spend the time of your entire life. You know this ability as choice. You can choose *anything*. You choose *everything*.

Ignorance is a choice; so is learning. Misery is a choice; so is joy. Unforgivingness is a choice; so is forgiving. You choose disease, fear, stagnation, or you choose health, love, growth. You choose according to what you believe.

It is not what you *experience* that forms what you *believe*, but what you *believe* that forms what you *experience*. Beliefs cause results, experience being a natural result. If the experiences of your life are not producing what you desire, then *believe differently*. What you experience will be different, producing what you do desire.

A time arrives in your life—at any age—when you realize that *you* decide what you believe, when you realize that *what* you believe has *consequences*. This connection to your conscious decision-making process contains the power of living the life you desire to live. When you deny or ignore this connection, you deny and ignore the power you possess.

In the past, you always did decide what you believe—but you did not understand, or else denied or were unaware of the fact. Once you become aware, you can no longer blame your parents, your teachers, your church, your spouse, your poverty, your disease, or any outside influence for what you believe and for the consequences of your beliefs. You—and you alone—are responsible. This does not always keep you from seeking someone to blame and avoid-

Take your life in your own hands and what happens? A terrible thing: no one to blame.

ERICA JONG

ing responsibility, but once mindful of your ability to choose, you fool only yourself when you do not activate your ability to choose.

If you decide to believe as a bigot, then you reap the consequences that bigotry renders, which is what you wish. If you decide to believe as a loving person, then you gain the rewards that a life of love gives, which is what you wish. If you decide not to forgive so-and-so, then you believe that person unworthy of your forgiveness, and the consequences perpetuate your unhappiness. If you decide to forgive so-and-so, then you believe that person worthy of your forgiveness, and the consequences produce positive growth.

But another's worth should never be questioned. Not judging means accepting another as a fellow human, equal to you as a child of the Universe. If you are one with the Source, so is the person you judge—and then you judge the Source. Realize you are not the only one searching for love. The person you desire to forgive is also searching for love. You are in the same boat. Why not help each other paddle to the shore of love?

What about others' beliefs, opinions, or judgments of you? What do you feel when you listen to someone criticize you? There are different contexts of criticism, but no matter which and no matter the source, its only value is what you concede to the criticism. Again, *you* decide where you place your focus.

Choosing what to believe does not advocate denial nor devalue others' opinions. If people and circumstances constantly give you information about a particular fault, you can choose to ignore these criticisms. But in your silence, when you look deep within, which criticism has truth in it for you? How would you like to clean up that behavior? What would you like to *believe* differently in order to *behave* differently in order to *achieve* differently?

If in your silence the judgments ring false to your sense of what is true, then you must stand firm and resolute. First, *know* your truth, then *accept* it, then *believe* in your truth. Faced with adversity, you achieve results because of courage, because of a stubborn refusal to reject the truth of what you think, do or say. Pay attention to the voice inside, to your innate sensibility. *Believe in your truth.*

With your desire to forgive may come the temptation to blame yourself. The beliefs you once held as truth may have hurt and harmed someone. You may feel bad or inept or uncaring. Self-judgment and self-criticism can zap your power as much as judging and criticizing others. Forgive yourself. Love yourself. If you ask yourself, "Why don't I love myself?" many times the answer is "Because I don't like who and what I am." Your dislike of someone else may simply be a mirror image of the very quality you exhibit and do not desire.

Accept yourself. Blaming your race, your physical challenge, your past—whatever you blame for your *perceived* imperfection—creates a smokescreen that keeps you from seeing your truth: your perfection. It is easy to say, "Deal with it," or "Get over yourself," but in essence this is what you must do. Do so lovingly, gently, forgivingly. If you do not accept yourself or terminate issues that keep you from loving yourself and others, there is always a cosmic kick in the pants to urge you on your way. Change what you believe.

Darkness is cheap, and Scrooge liked it.

CHARLES DICKENS

No character ever received such a unique urge to change his belief system as dramatically as good old Mr. Scrooge. He believed that people were unlovable because he believed he was unlovable. The judgments of others and circumstances constantly gave Scrooge information that he was mean-spirited, selfish, and defective. These were the consequences of what he believed. He stood firm, resolute, and chose to ignore these criticisms. He denied his accountability, and in denying it, he denied his love and his truth, not only to others but to himself.

Only in the dead of night, in his silence, when Scrooge paid attention, did he finally accept himself and his past. Scrooge decided to change what he *believed*, which changed his *behavior*, which changed the *experiences* in his life from that day forward.

It was not too late.

Scrooge found—or rather rediscovered—his truth, his love for himself, his humanity. Suddenly love surrounded the old boy. In essence, Scrooge forgave himself and his past, and then moved on; but *he* made the choice—not the ghosts, not Mrs. Cratchit, not his nephew. And he did so with his whole heart.

Scrooge could have ignored and denied everything surrounding him and joined his partner Jacob Marley in spiritual limbo. Instead, he chose to ignore and deny the false appearances of his imperfection and the imperfection of the people around him. Those false appearances—they are the ghosts, the illusions that mask the truth of love in the heart of everyone.

It is never too late to change what you believe. You decide what is true about you. Self-inflicted and implied judgments and opinions carry the weight you give them. If you believe you are unworthy, you will behave as though you are unworthy. If you believe your race keeps you from succeeding, you will not succeed. If you believe your disease will kill you, you will die.

Life inundates you with information. This is why silence is so important. In it you allow yourself time to regroup, sort out, receive messages, and get clear. Later, you determine what is of value, what has meaning for you. You determine your own truth. You decide what you believe. If you do not like how your beliefs make you feel or the consequences of believing them—in other words, your beliefs are not bringing you joy, health, love, fulfillment—then believe differently.

Your real truth—which is that you are a child of the Universe and conceived out of Love as love—has never changed, will never change, and is present within you as you read this statement. The same is true about those you desire to forgive.

> *You must understand that you have done*
> *what you needed to do; it was all necessary.*
> *And you made all the right choices—*
> *all of them!*

RAMTHA

Prayer   Use this or write your own.

> To My Nameless Power Within:
> I don't know what to believe any more.
> I thought I knew how the world worked,
> But things aren't working for me
> The way I want them to work.
> Forces outside me tell me I'm wrong,
> But some things inside I know are right.
> Help me to see the difference.
> Help me to look into my heart
> And learn what I long to change
> And what I seek to keep.
> Remove blame and judgment from my heart.
> Fill the gaps with beliefs that bring what I really crave:
> Joy, happiness, fulfillment, peace, freedom, love.
> Deep within I know what these beliefs are.
> Help me uncover the light of my truth
> So that I might see the light of truth in others.
> Help me forgive myself
> So that I might forgive others.
> Amen.

Exercises   Answer any of these questions and statements in your notebook. If anything else comes to mind, write about that.

1. What do I believe about myself? About the world? About the subject I desire to forgive?
2. Knowing I would be 100 percent successful, if I could choose any negative quality in myself, which would I like most to change? What positive quality in myself would I like most to expand?
3. What old beliefs would I like to change? What new beliefs would I like to create? How do my beliefs prevent me from forgiving?
4. How do I judge other people? How do other people judge me? How do I judge myself? What negative or positive traits about myself do I deny? What is the most common criticism I hear about myself? Is it valid to me? Why?

Affirmations Write your own or use these suggestions.

1. I believe in the goodness of _____.
   My new belief brings forgiveness of
   _____. I am safe to believe this
   new thought at the very moment I think this
   new belief.

2. As I think this thought, I proclaim that I
   believe differently. I choose to believe in my
   goodness. I choose to believe in the goodness of _____. These new beliefs
   bring blessed relief, yet a new vitality en-
   ergizes my life. I am one with the Higher
   Energy of Life.

3. Today I learn to love; to love myself, to love
   all I come into contact with in my experiences
   during this wonderful day. I know that love
   returns to me tenfold. Any other reaction I
   let go of and turn over to my Greater Love.

In Silence Find your quiet. Use these suggestions. Ask or envision anything you choose. Record any observations.

1. I believe _____.
   What must I do to change my beliefs?
2. Why can I not let go of this belief? How can I let go of this belief?
3. Ask yourself for permission to let go of an old belief; then grant it with love.

My Declaration to Forgive

Add the italicized statements. If your feelings have changed, change that blank. Be creative! Add or change anything you desire. Make your changes positive.

Mother Goddess,
With this thought I align myself with You.
I know Your Power is the power within me.
I declare right here and now that I forgive _____.
I release my capacity to love _____.
At this very moment, I feel relief. My mind, body, and emotions relax. My heart fills with warmth, and I feel _____

_____.

I find and know the good of this experience.
I feel compassion toward _____.
Clear thinking is mine. I believe _____.
Peace and Freedom are mine.
Thank You for opening my mind and my heart.
I let go of this declaration and set loose the Power of the Universe.
Amen.

*A*ctively surrender to your self
and your Higher Self. You lose
nothing but fear. And you
gain everything that is love.

◆

*We believe that forms of worship do not
matter to the Great Spirit; what pleases
Him is the offering of a sincere heart.*

SA-GO-YE-WAT-HA

*For every one who says, "Speak, Lord,
thy servant heareth," there are ten who say,
"Hear, Lord, thy servant speaketh."*

MOTHER JULIANA OF NORWICH

Steps to Forgiving

6

Surrender

What is your purpose? To love, to give and get love. To express love toward others and receive love from others. To reveal your love in all you do and manifest it in all areas of your life. What other purpose could you possibly have?

Whether you feel worse, and curse the day you began the forgiving process, or feel you have triumphantly forgiven: surrender. This does not mean that you wave the white flag of capitulation, that you give up at the expense of your personality, that you lose. Quite the contrary. Desires, resistance, issues—the more of your self you surrender to your Higher Power, the more personal power you gain. Your nature expresses effortlessly. By surrendering, you win. Do not force more feeling or awareness. Faking it will get you nowhere.

Defeat claims no part of surrendering to your Higher Self. What you do give up, what you do wave the white flag about, is your need to control people and situations and outcomes. Your ego no longer holds your will hostage. You no longer attach to things of this plane but attune to the whispers of a Higher Plane. Constantly questioning the insecurities in your life converts to an unquestioning security in your Higher Life.

The surrender paradox follows the concept of the acorn and the oak. The acorn does not grow into an elm or a lamb or a woman. Everything needed for the acorn to grow into an oak already exists within the seed.

To parallel this idea, the complete person of you already lives within you—all your unique talents, love and natural yearnings. Everything you need to grow into the complete you already exists within you.

The idea of the complete person lives within everyone! But unlike the acorn, humans have choice.

Somewhere along the line of your life, you made choices which contradict your completeness. You struggle and resist and block the natural flow of your beingness, until you decide that frustration and dysfunction and grief are no longer sufficient. Then you get out of your own way. You begin to live the already living idea of the complete you. You complete yourself.

To love oneself is the beginning of a lifelong romance.

OSCAR WILDE

If you believe your Higher Power is responsible for your existence and placed you on this planet for a purpose, then It put the complete idea of you within you to fulfill that purpose. Why would It leave you here incomplete? Even if you do not believe this as such, you constantly reveal more of yourself to yourself. Call it life. Consequently, you express more of the you who already exists.

Who knows better what you desire to express and manifest than the Power of personal consciousness that placed these desires within you in the first place? Surrendering to your Higher Power or your own consciousness allows personal revelation, evolvement, expression. You were born limitless. You come full circle.

In both release (or letting go) and surrender, you invoke the help of your Higher Power. In both cases you affirm conscious statements so as to give orders to your unconscious. In both cases, you act as if the statemenets are fact and so you empower yourself.

How is surrender different from release?

RELEASE	SURRENDER
Specific	General
Intellectual	Emotional
Episodic	All-encompassing

Release deals with a distinct emotion, issue, or thing you wish to shed, change, resolve, or manifest. Release can be an emotional movement but suggests a mostly abstract act, certainly not uninvolved, because of course you have feelings about what you are releasing. But you transform these feelings into an intellectual statement within your conscious mind. Release tends to be singular, episodic, or event-driven.

Surrendering knows no boundaries. To really surrender requires an emotional investment because you yield your entire life to an

*I'm dying of thirst by
the side of the fountain.*

CHARLES D'ORLÉANS

entire *way* of life. This is an act for which
there are no words, only sensations from
the most intimate core of who you are:
your soul, your energy, your essence,
whatever you wish to call it.

To surrender is a willing transference of your individual power
to your Higher Power. You operate from the center of yourself,
intuit with greater awareness, make decisions with greater ease. Oh
yes, you still have will, you still make choices. Surrendering is not
a way of shirking your repsonsibilities, but a way to accept them.
And one of your responsibilities is to know your truth.

When you surrender, your resistance to your truth disappears.
You grow compliant, able to yield elastically when the sometimes
overwhelming forces of life pound upon you or when you are
choosing a door of opportunity. You are in the moment, in the
flow. Clarity of purpose rises effortlessly.

As described in Step 2, surrendering a problem to your Divinity does not mean that Divinity now has the problem. Divinity cannot comprehend problems. This is not in Its Nature. *You* are the

one with the problem—because you conceive it. Taking a problem to your Divinity means that you place faith in your own power to transform your thinking in order to solve the problem.

So if you end up using your own power, why do you need a Higher Power? Because It is your Source. Because you get your power from It. Because It is the Generator of the Universe.

To forgive another, to forgive yourself, constitutes a courageous effort to right your life, to align yourself with your Higher Self. Now is the time to release your decisions with more conviction, more enthusiasm, more love. Surrender to Spirit. Think of this step as *Let Go and Set Loose, Part Two,* only on a deeper level. But if you give up or stop this process, your decision is perfect. You can always pick up where you left off, and you have not failed.

No matter how you define your level of achievement, you have changed. Your participation may have been heart-felt or half-hearted, but you have received what you wanted to receive. If you think your change is small, you may actually have accomplished more than you realize. If you think your change is great, an issue you have not seen or dealt with or that you have ignored may lurk in your mind and threaten your progress. Next week, next year, in the next five minutes, as you change so will your definition of *how* you have changed.

If you are comfortable with this process and think you have forgiven, fantastic! Congratulations! Surrendering reinforces your comfort. All the good you feel has only just begun. But (not to rain on your parade) realize that as you peel away a layer of issues, more may surface. This is a natural progression of growth, but you are better equipped to handle it. If new issues surface, surrender them. If they do not, think of this step as double-checking your progress.

If discomfort hinders you and you are still in the throes of turmoil, this step repeats more deeply a process to acquire comfort. Know relief: that your decision to forgive is in Trusting Hands. Know confidence: that an incredible Force helps rid you of your misery. Now you can focus on your goals. Surrender until you achieve the results you desire.

In either case, practice makes perfect—or rather, reveals to you what is already perfect: you and your life.

Your decision to forgive may have dredged up a lot of long-buried garbage. Realizing that you have been in control all along, seeing what you allowed to happen, admitting what you have done and become: all of this can be a great shock. People hurt you with your permission. You hurt people out of fear. Do not let this new awareness sabotage your intentions. Let it be a catalyst toward fulfilling your intentions.

Surrender any new issues. Ignorance can no longer be an excuse for negative conditions to be present in your life. Flush out the gunk that plugs the natural flow of your power. Once uncovered, the congealed mass of misconceptions that lie hidden, despoiling your life and the lives of others, cannot withstand the light of your awareness. The brightness of your internal light and the Power of your Higher Light destroy any false appearances. Illusions vanish like the mist that shadows your sun, evaporating by high noon, revealing the sun that always shines. Forgive yourself and move on.

Take a leap of faith. Every time you do—a small leap or a great leap—your consciousness expands. And so does the world's. The issues that bring you and the world to forgiving disappear.

In order to gain a more purposeful life, return to your primary purpose. Surrender to the Divine Nature and unleash the vital Power of the Universe, the Force of Life Itself. Only by surrendering what appears to control you do *you* control *it*; only thus do you regain control of your life and your destiny. Giving up this battle does not result in chaos and captivity but a victory that champions peace and freedom. Now the bud of your being can flower naturally, effortlessly. Forgiving is simply the catalyst.

How do you know if you have truly surrendered? Take a look around you. You will know when you *know*.

In service, we taste unity.

RAM DASS

Prayer   Use this or write your own.

>Dear Silent Partner,
>Whenever I think of _____
>I still feel so angry, so worthless,
>Like I am being judged, hurt and harmed.
>I no longer wish to be a victim.
>Sometimes I hurt and judge other people.
>I no longer wish to be a persecutor.
>I do wish to stick with my decision to forgive
>
>_____.
>
>I seek to know his/her/its holy light.
>I seek to release my ugly feelings and my attachment
>   to them.
>I seek to recognize my perfection.
>I seek to recognize _____'s perfection.
>But at times I have more issues than when I started
>   to forgive.
>I feel like giving up, like this is not worth the effort.
>Help me to find the strength to continue.
>Help me to see and not sabotage the good I have achieved.

I have seen some light.
It's just that I keep running into things in the dark
   that still invade my heart.
I long only to see more light, the light of forgiveness.
I ask to accept myself and my feelings
   but release them when it is time.
I desire to trust that this forgiving is not harming me,
That it is not leading me down a false path.
Help me to see that by not forgiving I do go down a
   false path.
I try so hard, so very hard.
Light my way.
Light the way of the one I forgive.
Light the way to Your Light.
I surrender myself to myself.
I surrender myself to my Higher Self.
I surrender to You.
I release this prayer into Your Hands
And I unleash Your Power.
Amen.

Exercises   Answer any of these questions and statements in your notebook. If anything else comes to mind, write about that.

1. What have I successfully let go of? What more would I like to let go of?
2. Have I forgiven _____?
   If so, how do I feel? If not, what more do I need to do?
3. What has changed since I began my process to forgive?
4. What does control mean to me? How does letting go of controlling (or what seemingly controls me) give me control?
5. How have I harmed people? Do I need to forgive myself?
6. What does surrender mean to me?
7. What is the complete idea of me?

Affirmations   Write your own or use these suggestions.

1. I release my past. I renew my life with love and joy. I let go of _____.
   I forgive _____ right now and with my whole heart.
2. I announce to myself that I am in the flow. I surrender to Love. Together we flow toward all that is love, and all that is love flows toward me and from me.
3. Right now, I proclaim that I am a point of courage in the Power of my Divinity. I acknowledge the bravery of my heart as I forgive _____. I align myself with Spirit and surrender to the Universe. Only good surrounds me. Only good surrounds _____. This reality begins in this moment.

In Silence Find your quiet. Use these suggestions. Ask or envision anything you choose. Record any observations.

1. Picture yourself as a string of flexible, bright, white light. Picture a larger string of flexible, bright, white light. This is your Higher Power. Hitch a ride with It and go wherever you desire.
2. Invoke your Higher Power. State what you have released. State what remains. Ask for guidance. Ask what you need to surrender.
3. Picture the person you desire to forgive. See the subject as a shape of light and love. What does the light do or say?
4. Envision surrendering to your Higher Power. Envision the revelation and manifestation of the complete you.

My Declaration to Forgive

Add the italicized statements and further add or change anything
you desire. Make your changes positive.

Dear Heart,
With this thought I align myself with You.
I know Your Power is the power within me.
I declare right here and now that I forgive _____.
I release my capacity to love _____.
At this very moment, I feel relief. My mind, body, and
emotions relax. My heart fills with warmth, and I feel _____
_____.
I find and know the good of this experience.
I feel compassion toward _____.
Clear thinking is mine. I believe _____
_____.
Peace and Freedom are mine.
Thank You for being there to help.
I let go of this declaration and set loose the Power of the Universe.
My surrender is complete. Love flows from me and toward me.
I make this statement and know that it is so.
Amen.

*P*ut out your intentions. Let go.
The Universe can conceive of
much greater rewards. Let it!

◆

*Shoot for the moon. Even if you miss it,
you will land among the stars.*

LES BROWN

*When the soul wishes to experience some-
thing, she throws an image of the experience
out before her and enters into her own image.*

MEISTER ECKHART

Picture Your Perfect Peace;
Liberate Your Freedom

Finally, you start the last step! Your process nears completion, and the end is on the horizon. Have you truly forgiven the subject you decided to forgive?

If you answer yes, congratulations! If you answer no, congratulations! Either response is perfect for you.

No matter what you answer, the process never ends. The quest to forgive elevates your consciousness to a higher level of awareness. You evolve. You cannot return to ignorance. Deny your awareness and you risk the fulfillment of your life, your peace, your freedom. The stakes are very high.

You planted a seed which you nurtured. The seed sprouted and grew into what? You desired to forgive, to achieve peace and freedom. If you know what that looks like for you, you harvest the fruits of your labors. If you do not know what that looks like for you, cultivate your desires further. You must have an idea of what you desire to manifest in your life; then *identify* yourself with this idea in your mind.

It is false to say an absence of thought yields nothing. This is an impossibility, since you are *always* thinking something. That "something" demonstrates what happens to you in your life. *Direct* your thinking. *Choose* consciously what you place in your mind.

Manifestation of your desires does not rest solely on thinking. You must also do what you have to do to forgive, to achieve peace and freedom. Walk your talk. Move your feet. Other actions distract you from your goals.

Peace is balance, wholeness, harmony, security, a mental state of calm, quiet and tranquillity. Picture your perfect peace. How do you desire to express peace in your life?

Freedom is a mental and physical absence of restriction. Being free

Freedom lies in bold action.

ROBERT FROST

means being at ease, open, bold of concept and execution. Before you can liberate your freedom, define it. What do you desire to be free of or to do?

Peace and freedom are yours for the asking—but *know* what you ask for. Tap your imaginaton. Have some fun! Play the game of "What Do I Want My Life to Look Like?" Go wild, be frisky and risky, frolic in your mind. Only *you* limit your creativity. Once you allow your imagination to run wild, to picture what you desire, you have a more tangible goal. Your desires form and take shape. If you have no idea what you want, pay attention to your instinct, intuition, those "inklings." They light the way toward self-discovery.

Peace and freedom are not dependent on forgiving; and even if you have not totally forgiven the subject you decided to forgive, you can still play this game. There are no rules. But you will know greater peace and greater freedom *through forgiving*. Why settle for less?

Allow a natural unfolding. Put out your intention, and let the Universe take Its Own Course in Its Own Good Time—not yours.

Your dream may look totally different from what you thought, and it may manifest beyond even your wildest imagination. Let go of appearances, of controlling how reality materializes. The Universe can conceive of much greater things than you. Let It!

Do not worry about results. Worry is creative imagination used negatively. Play, peace, gladness, and fun: these are the results of creative imagination used positively.

All that is in your life begins by a thought and ends in a consummation of your consciousness.

Do you rule your consciousness with prosperity? Think and feel abundance and boundless potential—and you experience overflow and bounty. *You* define the prosperity: twenty bucks or a million dollars; a restful night of sleep; a new car, house, career; a bouquet of flowers; health; a loving relationship or a pleasant date.

Do you rule your consciousness with poverty? Think and feel lack and limitation—and your experience will mirror your pattern of thought: unhappiness in the midst of plenty, abusive relationships, dissatisfying jobs, illness, an empty bank account.

Change the habits of your mind. They may not exit easily.

Personal issues raised may cling to your consciousness and may not readily accept cutting. Recognize that you seek to say good-bye to thoughts that have occupied your mind and life for however long. You have spent much time and energy coddling their presence, justifying and protecting them.

Your entire identity may be tied up with your issues. Once you resolve them, you may fear the void that remains. But what an exciting opportunity awaits you! You get to choose what you put in your internal space! Instead of miseries, see what marvels you now can create with your time and energy.

When you consciously think what you seek to think and experience the joys this supplies, you may wonder why you did not do this before now. Do not berate yourself. Do not let a new habit sabotage your efforts to forgive, to manifest your desires. You accomplish what you accomplish with perfect timing. Compare yourself to no one. *No one!* You are you, unique and perfect and loving. Celebrate that fact!

it takes courage to grow up and turn out to be who you really are

e. e. cummings

The Universe knows your truth, knows who you are, knows your talents. It should. It put them there—with great love. Your job is to discover your gifts and express them. The Universe is not keeping them a secret from you; *you* are. The idea of the oak is in the acorn. In other words, the expression of the seed is already complete within the seed. And so it is with you. The expression of you is already complete within you.

But what lies dormant within you? What ideas drive you to desire expressing them, and why do you not express them? The ideas were placed there with great purpose: to allow you—this marvelous, one-of-a-kind embodiment of love—to manifest these ideas in your life.

For example, you know you have always aspired to be a writer or a builder. How do you know? Because an urge consciously rises in your mind and your heart. You wrote little poems in junior high or played wtih wooden blocks as a child, and these acts brought you great joy. But somewhere along the line of your life, fears crept in and prevented you from pursuing your talents. You were sidetracked, and instead of following your natural path, here you are on a detour rife with the potholes of unhappiness and unfulfillment. Realize that a detour is only that: a *temporary* deviation from a natural course. Engaging this process of forgiving puts you back on course. You possess the power to pursue your dreams and fulfill the completeness that is yours to express.

Feeling the good and the lightness that forgiveness brings reinforces your desire for more of the same. You find more and more time to fill your mind with thoughts of your choice. What will you put in the place of your anger, your fear, your apathy? Fill those vacancies with thoughts of freedom and peace and joy and light and love. Decide what these concepts and emotions should look like in your life. What does freedom look like? Peace? Joy? Love?

Everything you experience represents a stop before you step into the next moment, the next day, the next decade of your life. One follows the other with natural precision. This chapter of your life may not conclude to your satisfaction. You are the only one you need to satisfy, so you are the ultimate arbiter. Work until you are satisfied. Play until you are satisfied, and realize satisfaction may come from simply being. Freedom, peace, joy, love: these toys no one can take from you.

The process of forgiving touches every aspect of your life, not just forgiving. Thinking is a way of living. It requires constant maintenance because humans can easily return to old habits. But if you place your faith in yourself and your Higher Power, the maintenance strengthens your resolve to find what you desire to find. The foundation of your life builds on the constancy of your thought, creating a synergy that knows no bounds.

To attain forgiveness, vengeance and blame must be absent from your consciousness. To attain peace, confusion and disquiet must be absent from your consciousness. To attain freedom, limitation and timidity must be absent from your consciousness. You must not think the lesser and expect to get the greater.

The good you seek beats within you. This is your truth, always present, always available. Call upon it, and you cannot help but see the good that surrounds you. The heart's glad purpose is to respond with love, and peace and freedom are yours for the asking.

> *You never enjoy the world aright . . . till you perceive*
> *yourself to be the sole heir of the whole world.*
>
> THOMAS TRAHERNE

Prayer   Use this or write your own.

> Dear Great Love,
> I think I'm finally understanding.
> But there are still some habits that cause me grief.
> Take me beyond myself.
> Take me to the place where my imagination flies,
> Where instead of timid I am bold,
> Where instead of chaos I find quiet.
> Show me that the trust and security I desire lie within.
> Give me the courage to choose what I desire.
> I know this will happen.
> Give me the patience to be easy on myself.
> Open my heart and let the sun of Your Light shine
>   on me.
> To love and be loved is all I desire.
> Thank You,
> Amen

Exercises Answer any of these questions and statements in your notebook. If anything else comes to mind, write about that.

1. What do I want my life to look like?
2. What do peace and freedom look like to me? Joy? Love? How can I play to manifest these toys in the re-creation of my life?
3. What tells me I have a poverty consciousness? A prosperity consciousness?
4. Write a letter to your fears. Acknowledge them, state what good they provided you in your life, say goodbye to them, state what you are replacing them with.
5. If you have forgiven the subject you decided to forgive, write a letter of congratulation to yourself. If you have not, write a letter of congratulation to yourself complimenting yourself on what you have accomplished.

Affirmations   Write your own or use these suggestions.

1. I know at this very moment my imagination soars. I realize all that I desire. Forgiveness, peace and freedom are mine.
2. Today, I channel my mind, heart and spirit to my greater Spirit. All that is good comes to me, all love, all prosperity. I give all good, love, and wishes for prosperity to all I touch today.
3. I state that my efforts to forgive _____ are complete. I celebrate my efforts. I celebrate with a knowing quiet, secure in my trust of myself and my Higher Power. The lightness I feel brings peace and freedom and I know that this is so at the very heart of my soul.

4. At the moment I think this, peace of mind is mine. I smile, knowing that balance and harmony go with me wherever I go and touch all I touch. Spirit guides me always. I declare that the freedom I feel creates a boldness within, and my imagination has no boundaries. Today anything is possible.

In Silence Find your quiet. Use these suggestions. Ask or envision anything you choose. Record any observations.

1. In my mind I see a playground. A companion appears and together we decide what to play.
2. What do peace and freedom look like? Where do I find peace and freedom? Picture it. Locate it.
3. What do I want my life to look like? How do I get there? Receive direction.

My Declaration to Forgive

Add the italicized statements. Make any changes you desire. Make them positive. Fill in the new blanks to accomplish or experience. Be creative! Let go and set loose YOURSELF!

O Nameless Force of Mine!
With this thought I align myself with You.
I know Your Power is the power within me.
I declare right here and now that I forgive _____.
I release my capacity to love _____.
At this very moment, I feel relief. My mind, body, and emotions relax. My heart fills with warmth, and I feel _____

_____ .

I find and know the good of this experience.
I feel compassion toward _____.
Clear thinking is mine. I believe _____

_____ .

My peace is _____.
I am free to _____.
Thank You for my growth. Thank You for this experience.

I let go of this declaration and set loose the Power of the Universe.
My surrender is complete. Love flows from me and toward me.
I make this statement and know that it is so.
Amen.

Now What?

Where is happiness in hopelessness? Where is the party in pity? Where is creativity in mediocrity? Where is confidence and honor in arrogance and shame? Where is compassion in malice? Where is amusement in remorse? Where is enthusiasm and ecstasy in apathy? Where is joy, blessing, and generosity in stinginess and selfishness? Where is enchantment in disgust? Where is friendship in jealousy and envy?

The greatest part of our happiness or misery depends on our dispositions and not on our circumstances.

MARTHA WASHINGTON

Where is discovery in justification? Where is forgiving in punishment, freedom in bondage, peace in strife? Where is love in hate?

Nowhere! This is not news. This is not rocket science. Yet, at one time or another, in the past or right now, all of us experience the negative side of life, proclaiming loudly that we desire the positive. So why does the negative show its black shadow in our lives? *Because we choose to allow its presence in our lives.*

You are told by television and radio, the newspaper, in books, in church, and in art, what the good life should look like: you should be in shape and beautiful; you should have the latest car, clothes, and compact disk; you should believe this or that, eat this pasta because it is better than that one—and on and on and on, until your brain cannot help but short-circuit.

People who buy into these appearances give you feedback: you are not pretty enough, do not drive a nice car, have a lousy job, wear ugly clothes—as though you are your body, your Ford, your job, your pants. At times it is no wonder you do not know what to think.

There is nothing wrong wtih getting good things to enhance your life and make it better, but what is in your heart? If your heart does not sing at some point in your day, no appliance, soap, or battery will charge it: it's up to you.

But you are not alone.

Where is Spirit in your world? Do you recognize and acknowledge the Force within you? Do you use it to create the positive you proclaim you desire?

Life can be ugly. Life can be difficult. Life can blast us with a thousand pieces of information making our head spin trying to assimilate it all. People are mean. People do bad things. People hurt us, and we in turn hurt back.

The purpose of life is love—to give it and get it. Nothing else motivates the human. The basic needs of food, clothing and shelter motivate self-preservation, which is still self-love. Every action you engage is motivated by love. *Every one!*

You were born as an expression of love—the Love of the Life Force. You were born peaceful and free. Somewhere along the way, you made choices that contradicted your original plan. Now you search to return to your purpose.

Only by letting go of the past can you gain control of your present and future. Controlling the very thing that appears to control you lies in giving yourself up to it.

If you truly wish to forgive, to be free of the person who you think enslaves you, embrace him, release him, love him. It is easy to find fault with people. The challenge is to find *their perfection*! As a child, you gazed at the world through innocent eyes and saw perfection naturally. The need to search for it indicates eyes that have become clouded with cataracts of fear. Excise these "cataracts" with love.

Love! Love! Love! What a beautiful word, yearned for by all yet so commonly unpracticed. The love of a dog is unconditional. The love of a child is unconditional. The Love of God is unconditional. Why withhold *your* love? Be like the puppy. Be like the child who lives within you. Be like God. Yes! Be like God! After all, you possess the same traits. Use them. Oil the rusty floodgates of your heart and let your love flow forth unconditionally so that it may rush back to you unconditionally.

You have been willing to explore the extent of your fears and hatreds and low self-esteem. Now is the time to explore the extent of the love you have to give to yourself, your enemies, your world. That may present a different set of tasks more formidable than your exploration of forgiving, but, as with this process, you gain nothing by not risking.

To forgive is to heal. Forgive, and you heal yourself. Any effort you make to forgive propels you toward fulfilling your potential as a joyfully and lovingly empowered human being. Collectively, everyone's efforts to forgive propel the world toward fulfilling its potential as a joyful and loving planet of wondrous power. When you heal, the world heals—and the world is in great need of healing.

Never underestimate the power of your healing. Individual evolution yields social revolution with the firepower of love. Witness the works of Gandhi and Martin Luther King, Jr.

While it is true that you have used some Power to attain forgiveness, it is also true that this same Power can use *you* to be of service to humankind. What would you like to give back to the world? Your service need not be grandiose, for in the most mundane deed lies the holiest nugget of Love's eternal grace. No effort motivated by love is trivial.

Be a wondrous instrument of beautiful change. Beginning in your mind, forgiving happens in your heart. When you live love, effort becomes needless because the causes of forgiving no longer exist. Life and love become effortless.

Commit this act of love this moment, for this moment is truly all you have. And as you read these words, the moment has already passed. Better to have relished it! Better to have lived it! Better to have loved it!

Bottom line: you forgive when you understand there is no one and no thing to forgive.

Do all the good you can,
In all the ways you can,
To all the people you can,
In every place you can,
As long as ever you can.

THE SHAKERS

Exercises   Answer any of these questions and statements in your notebook. If anything else comes to mind, write about that.

1. How have my discomforts been ''blessings of inestimable value''?
2. How have I healed?
3. How have I helped heal the world?
4. How would I like to be of service?
5. What truths am I pretending not to know?
6. In my life is there no one or no thing I need to forgive?

In Silence Find your quiet. Repeat these thoughts or envision them appearing on a blank, white screen.

BE.
Be still.
Be still and know.
Be still and know that I AM.
Be still and know that I AM GOD WITHIN YOU.
Be still and know that I AM.
Be still and know.
Be still.
BE.

Thanksgiving

Life itself is the proper binge.

JULIA CHILD

Sarah and Reuben: For being the most wonderful, kind, intelligent, talented, giving, and loving people a child ever had the good fortune of calling Mom and Dad.

Mile Hi Church of Religious Science, Denver, Colorado: Thank you for being a sanctuary of peace and freedom and love and empowerment and fulfillment.

Rev. Scott Schell, Unity minister: For his wonderful talk on Forgiving, June 7, 1996, at the Gay and Lesbian Spiritual Support Group of Mile Hi Church.

Dr. Robert Brumet: For inspiring Scott at a lecture presented at the Unity School of Christianity in Missouri.

Lee, Eric, Tom, Dan: For nudging me with love-shoves.

Kagey, Mitch, Tom, Johnny V., Michael, Marco, George, Archie, Paul, Tony, Jeff: Though all of you are on a fantastic cruise of the cosmos, you still repose in a cozy corner of my heart. I would not be here today if not for your lessons and love.

Come to the edge, he said.
They said, We are afraid.
Come to the edge, he said.
They came.
He pushed them . . .
And they flew.

GUILLAUME APOLLINAIRE

Colorado aids Project: For the Grief Group and facilitators Ralph McFadden and Ron Villadao, who put me back on the path of life.

The Experience: For putting me back on the path of love.

Gary Peattie and Arthur Vergara: For their guidance in bringing this book to light.

Joel Fotinos, publisher: For encouraging me and thinking of me and this book.

Anyone I have ever come into contact with in my life: Just covering all the bases.

Me: For not giving up. It is no longer in my nature.

Spirit: For never giving up on me. It is not in Your Nature, never was, never will be.

COMMENTS OR QUESTIONS? YOU MAY REACH MR. KITZMAN VIA e-MAIL AT:

spivMan@ix.netcom.com